# Through the Shards of My Heart

By Machelle Berglund

# Table of Contents

## Love in Those Angsty Days  Page 8
- Young, Angsty Love
- Denied Myself a Snack
- As Long as Your Heart is Beating
- A Piece of a Dream
- Labyrinthe Love
- Only a While
- Dream of Never
- Silks of Our Stolen Moments
- Me Vs. Her
- Silly Little Things
- Meat on a Hook
- Burn Me Alive
- Flow Through

## Here's to Hoping  Page 34
- Here's to Hoping
- I'll Sit With You
- Like a Moth to a Flame
- Boys with Brown Eyes
- Decisions on Doors
- "Nice"
- Maybe
- Attention
- Pretend
- Unrequited

*Be Bold*
*Breath Reads Salty*
*Little Shelf in My Heart*

*Hollyhock for Your Heart*
*Drunken Text*
*Preference*

## Broken Love  *Page 58*

*When Hearts are Broken*
*They Whisper*
*For the Sake of You*
*Once Upon a time*
*Crash*
*Wings*
*Shut Your Mouth*
*A Million Reasons*
*Heart Eater*
*Into Dust*
*The Inevitable*
*Finished Plate*
*Sweet Tea*
*Through the Shards of My Heart*
*Drunken Knight*
*Meant to Be*

## Letting the Love Be  *Page 84*
- *Love, At Last!*
- *I Found You*
- *Don't Want the Music to Stop*
- *Walking in the Rain*
- *Triskeles*
- *Hearth*
- *Reassurance*
- *Locks*
- *Green Love*
- *Vulnerability*
- *Let the Love Be*
- *To the Women I've Loved*
- *My Adonis*
- *Your Patience*

## Acknowledgements and Notes  *Page 103*
## About the Author  *Page 105*

Dedicated to Mr. Tim and Mrs. Schnieder of Baltic Elementary.

This will be one of many books dedicated to you two. Thank you for all that you did for me.

# Love in Those Angsty Days

When love, angst, and poetry collide during those teenaged years

## Young, Angsty Love

In the days of my youth,
when I walked
alongside you
in a dark parade,
my heart became afflicted
by young, angsty love

And with the spread of the
affliction,
I wrote poetry and songs
and I climbed the various
heights of the hawthornes,
hoping to cure my heart
of that damnable curse,
that young, angsty love

But no matter how I tried,
I couldn't escape the fate
set before me,

I couldn't escape falling into
a young, angsty love

Those chemicals in the mind
turned me towards romance,
and against them, my senses
failed,
nothing could avail me
of young, angsty love

I tried to say anything against
it,
to fight my teenage self
against the need to find a
paramore,
to focus on other things,
instead of pining away
for one boy after another,
but nothing could save me
from young, angsty love

## Denied Myself a Snack

I denied myself a snack,
to take a taste
of the sweet kiss of your lips,
and started to starve

I denied myself a sip,
to take a drink
of the warm nectar
that pours from your heart,
and started to suffer from
dehydration

I denied myself a chance
to dine with you,
although I was so hungry for your
love
as I believed
that my presence would poison
all your food

## As Long as Your Heart is Beating

The rose that you are,
a man that grew from a
barely budding flower,
forever fearing you'll
never get another solid hour,
Before you set away your
swinging swords known as doubt,
scream out loud those words
our hearts adore,
I want to open you up,
to hear those letters pour

Even if your head isn't level,
for neither is mine,
I just need to know if
you're still with me,
if you're even alive.

If your heart is no longer
beating....
Then no longer will mine.

## A Piece of a Dream

A piece of a dream,
that's all I really need,
a figure with warm hands
and a warm heart,
to thaw the spikes of ice
that grow in my heart,
to remind me that not
all is bitter cold,
that I am not made of
only snow

A sweet little hope,
that's all I can wish for,
sung in rosy breaths
that bitter days have gone by,
that the blizzards have ceased,
that the flowers will bloom,
and the trees will awaken,
that we can walk hand in hand
in this piece of a dream
without freezing in place
Just a bit of reality,
that's all I can try to remember,
enough to shake me down
another level, to dream some other
dream full of promises and loyalties
that this lonely heart
could share with another,
together we could dream our way
through the down and outs

life always seems to bring

I feel that I may wait centuries
in my wasted state of mind
to work my way to a worthier
state of being,
to be what I wished to be,
to feel as though I were worthy
of the pieces of these dreams,
I feel as though I shot for the
moons of spring,
and landed upon the fading stars
of winter

I am no Guinevere, nor Juliette,
Yet sire, you are by far my
Lancelot.
My knight, my dream, my fire,
the very light in the heavens that
wakes me from
a night's miserable slumber
and carries me upon the rays
of the morning sun into
a happier state of dreaming

A piece of you,
that's all I can hope to grasp,
as I wait,
living my life within
the pieces of my dreams,
working to control
the winters of my heart

## Labyrinthine Love

I had once thought
you were so charming.
Your labyrinthine eyes
had me in a world of
constant twists and turns,
magic was no longer
a myth nor a whisper,
but common practice

I yearned and searched
for the heart of your city,
hoping to reach it
to claim a stake for myself,
but tricks and traps
were at every turn,
for my suffering,
you didn't seem too concerned

I danced at your masquerades,
awkwardly, tripping over my skirts
Your cronies laughed,
and behind the mask,
you stifled an evil grin,
When you finally approached me,
you told me you couldn't let me go
and twirled me around and around

Your crystal images
gave me hope,
your kisses gave me butterflies,
your roses made me believe
in your lies


When I finally found
the truth of your illusions,
I left your city of
starlight and stone,
sickened by the maze
and the games I had to play
to feel even a glimmer of your
love

You always thought
you could win,
standing over me
as yet another kingdom
that you've conquered,
but in the end,
you had no real power over me

## Only a While

The morning star's light
has shined its last dawn
before collapsing into a black
hole,
vanishing from sight,
sucking in light,
leaving behind debris
that forms other planets, other
stars

The tree sheds the last
of its leaves
while winter hums
an icy lullaby,
leaving it asleep for a season,
but only a season,
the sun still rises,
and one day, the flowers come
back,
in full bloom

The little bird had
sung its last song,
before bursting into
feathers and blood
at the shot of a gun,
yet the other birds

still sing
and carry on,
scattering to other trees,
and singing on

The girl wipes away
the last of her tears
over the boy who had
burned a black hole
into her heart,
whose pretty little songs
were stuck in her head,
who was inconsolable for a while,
but only a while

For there are other stars in the sky,
other songs to sing,
other seasons in which to live,
and other people to love

## A Dream of Never

I've seen a face within
the curling mists of the morning,
the ghost of a man
I had never met
whose arms will never hold me,
whose lips I will never feel
against the nape of my neck,
whose princely voice will never
rattle my heart's inner ear

A phantom trapped behind the
glass,
A handsome dream kept
within the cloaks of mystique,
a visage that's nothing more than
never,
a man made by dream

## Silks of our Stolen Moments

The face of your name
Is eternally engraved
Within my tree bark of my heart,
while the webs that you wove
from the silks of our stolen
moments,
are tangled in the branches,
keeping a hold of all those
silly little words and phrases
we'd say,
the glimmer of your eyes catching
mine,
the sound of you playing guitar,
your notes dancing off the strings

For the time we had together,
It seemed as if it was all
but a dream themed drink
sealed inside a
bottle labeled "false hope",
guarded by malicious creatures
and other dark things that hide
deep in the dismal night,
and yet, I managed to steal
a vial almost every night

Though it was a potion of
illusions,

I couldn't stop myself from
sipping,

I couldn't stop myself from hoping
until that damnable night
those ghoulish arachnids appeared,
searching for the
lost treasures of
what we wanted to be

They left in their stead the
truths of what we really were,
of what was to come

I wanted to
forever be within your presence,
if anything, to be the
shade found beneath a tree,
granting shelter from the
sweltering sun,
or, if anything, a ghost within
your
always flowing thoughts,
drifting through as a friendly
spirit
on whom you could depend,
but now I know it will never be
so...

To get away from this place,
to escape before the spiders
possess and conquer our

beloved tangle of memory

means sacrifice,
means one of us gets left behind,
foolishly protecting what
should have been let go

I had hoped that you could help me
defeat the dark ones,
those eight-legged freaks
who taunt and torture,
and that you would remain to be the
good monster you claim to be,
but in those final moments,
you showed your true form,
and that's when I knew
I couldn't expect a monster
to ever be good

Only a couple threads from
the silks of our stolen moments
remain,
changed by time,
twisted,
with little shimmer left

While I still clutch onto them,
my grip is not as tight,
and the spiders no longer
taunt me as they used to

## Me Vs Her

I may not be a strong summer breeze
like she may be,
but my stench will blow you over,
that I can guarantee

Instead of the sweet bits
of flowers wafting on by,
I am a perfume of a
grandfather's coat left in
the basement closet
for years upon years,
the scent of mothballs
and musk surround my awkward self

Lemonade radiates off
her pleasant breath,
adding an element of fresh to
every kiss,
Unfortunately, the best I can do
is fill your mouth with
the tastes of onions and sugary cola
through an exchange of saliva,
but you're my lucky number one,
so pucker up sweetheart,
get ready for bliss

And though I'm less than
rosey in looks,
lacking a pleasant smile,
forever having a dead twinkle
shining out from my eyes,
I have funny faces
to entertain you all day,

Her smile makes all the pain go
away,
but I've got one better,
one that causes a laugh
to burst pass your lips
albeit there may also form
a slight discomfort in your soul

And her skin is so silky soft
and warm to the touch,
While I have lizard hide scales
serving as my epidermis,
my hands are always clammy,
my feet always cold

And yeah,
I've got to admit,
she's got the voice of an angel
that's always accompanied by
the likings of a harp,
but I've got the making of
a raptor screech that'll
rupture your drums,
and cause bleeding in the brain

Honestly, what more could you
want?

Sure, she's wonderful
and just as fun,
lacking major flaws on the
surface,
she's supportive, honest,
responsible,
doesn't hide her emotions
in a bottle tucked in way deep
and out of reach,
she's a heartful lover
full of adventure and happiness

Well, I'm full of adventure too,
though the roads I travel
are through haunted forests
full of gnarled trees,
and streets shrouded in mists
and darkness,
teeming with little creatures
that snip and bite,
I could be all those things,
one day, if given the time

She's a cool glass of spring
water,
healthy and reliable,
something sought after and needed,
but I am a hearty nip of whisky,

leaving you with the spins,
unable to process what had
happened
the night before

I don't mean to make this a thing
about me versus her,
but I'm just letting you know
that you've got options,
if you choose her,
you may find the bits
of yourself that you've been
missing,
but with me,
you could go on a wild ride
that may break you down
and make you rebuild yourself
from the ground up

The choice is yours,
it's either me,
or her

## Silly Little Things

Girls like me are such foolish
things
with high hopes bursting out
of their chests like ballerina
ribbon,
only for it to be ripped away,
by everyday things that grab on
tight
and yank it away with grimy hands,
but that is just a normal thing

What odd little creatures,
jumping off diving boards made of
glitter glue and dollar store
jewels,
expecting to land in a pool
of diamond dust,
instead hitting an ocean
of ice-cold reality,
diving down towards the rocky
bottom,
headfirst, making contact,
giving themselves several
instances of brain damage

Yes, they are silly little things,
pretending they have
butterfly wings and
starry bright eyes,
and with those wings,

they can soar high,
and others will
always compliment them
on the color of their irises.

They hold close a rosebud
that they hope will someday
blossom
inside their puppy dog hearts,
believing their true beauty
to show through
by the power and hue
of those pretty little petals

Girls are such strange things,
finding their optimisms
in the bottom of a perfume bottle,
their sweet smells drifting
upon a spring evening breeze,
causing a stir within
as it travels through your lungs
and to the center of your mind,
disguised as a scent,
though really soldiers battling
to conquer your brain before
rival warriors start their assault,
they leave behind such carnage in your heart
should you have been so unlucky
to fall in love with these silly little things

## Meat on a Hook

I put myself out there
like meat on a hook,
hoping to catch your attention,
to catch your hunger

Little did I know
that your appetite had
already been sated
by tastier things

I didn't get a bite,
not even a nibble

## Burn Me Alive

```
The inferno is ever reaching
within the intensity of your stare
it's flames licking away at my
skin,
peeling away layer after layer
until I am but bare bones

You burn me alive day by day,
yet only I am to blame
for becoming but a smokey haze
For I never step out of blaze
```

# Flow Through

They say that the love
should flow through and through,
and never stop,
and yet I cannot justify why
I try to hide away all the love
when all I want to do
is hold onto you

I want to give it
a chance,
to let it flow through
the dry, black veins
that starve for your refreshing
touch,
to let your essence wrap
around me and embrace me
with flowering vines pulsing
with a healing serum
full of love

I know I must scrounge
up the courage in any way I can,
to open the gateways,
light the paths,
and let you in,
to let you flow through,
I just don't know if I can,
if I am even able
to stop hiding away
all the love I feel for you

# Here's to Hoping

*Poems about introspection and the hope of find love*

## Here's to Hoping

It's taken me some time
to figure out what I want,
taken me quite some
time to process my thoughts

Emotions never came easy for me,
I always stuffed them down
any time they've tried
to rear their ugly heads,
sometimes before I even
know what I could have possibly felt

But now I know a little better,
and I'm starting to learn
that it's okay to feel,
to express,
and now I know
what I want…

And what I want is you.

Here's to hoping that you want me too…

# I'll Sit with You

You don't have to sit alone
on a bench of cold,
and let the snow cover you,
I'll sit by your side
for as long as I can,
until you're ready to get up

I know it's not easy,
living in a world
lacking in warmth,
but fires in the heart
can still start

You may think your flame
has forever quelled,
but I can see the embers within,
still glowing, still hot

I'll sit with you until
we can figure out
how to rekindle the blaze,
we'll keep trying,
taking it one day at a time

It may seem like
the snow will never quit,
but I'll be here all this time,
you won't have to sit alone
on this bench of cold

## Like a Moth to a Flame

I miss you like I miss
the smell of a midsummer's rain,
the sweet taste of angel cake,
and the feel of kisses
against my skin,
and I miss the way
your presence seems
to spirit away
vampiric thoughts of the past

I reach for you,
with the want of a dreamer
who wishes upon the stars,
with hands out and open,
hoping to touch
their twinkling beauty,
and I reach for you
like an artist reaches for
their muse to find the
pearls of inspiration
to create a work of art
that resembles the
beauty in your heart

And I yearn for you
like a restless spirit
yearns for adventure,
daring to dig for treasure
in silvery sands
where your love may lay

And I'm attracted to you
like a moth to the flame,
only the flame is the warm,
gentle caress of your hand,
and the fire in your eyes

## Boys with Brown Eyes

Damn those beautiful
boys with their brown eyes,
captivating my wandering mind
by the flash of their
amber lamplights as they
switch my way.
Unfortunately, their bulbs
burn out not long after
they spot me

Damn their heat rays
of the sepia sciences,
causing me to melt
into a puddle of bumbles
and nervous laughs.
When I finally solidify,
a part of me always remains
in a liquid state,
sloshing noisily upon
seeing those baby browns
emerge from underneath
skin-type beaker lids

And damn you most of all,
for it is your optics,
your orbs of dark honey tunnels
with lanterns at the end,
that pierce the veil of bone
that serves as my skull
coating my dendrites

with the taint of flowery notions
and words of romance,
letting slip past an
illusion of chance.

They travel through my head,
day and night,
using little wings
to bring my way
the pain of bee stings
                        that bring about
a constant
swelling in my brain.
The pus won't drain away

I just can't seem to
get those pretty eyes
out of my mind…

## Decisions on Doors

I half wish I could close that door,
too afraid to turn back
to face the past,
too afraid to face the
intimacy of the future.
It's not that anything would happen,
but there's always a "could"
and a "what if" hinging
off the bolts,
and taking hold in
the thin lumber grains
and cheap metal scraps,
trapped within a little squeak
of the door's opening creak,
those possibilities being
a long-time resident of the keyhole

It scares me.
More than any
monster I've ever faced.

Yet, if I closed that door,
even though it's barely cracked,
I know that the breath
I've held all these ages
will finally expire,
forcing its way out of my mouth,
through my lips,
and into the air,
never again to be mine


Still, I teeter on my advance...
Dare I push this door further
or let my lungs collapse?

## "Nice"

I accept that I'm
never the one to
cause your heart to pound,
out of your chest,
feeling yourself unbound,
so close to exploding
and imploding all at once

I know I could never
be the one you want and need,
not from a lover's happenstance
Though I wish it was more,
a friend is better than nothing….
and if I truly cared,
I'd be there to help you up
when you're down

My admirations I'll channel
in other ways,
instead of giving them out
like unwanted gifts
with no return slips,
I'll push away any thoughts
of entitlement to your affections

I don't ever want to be
a "nice" person
who does things for you
out of the expectation
that one day we'll
end up together,
that you'll realize
that I was "the one"
all along

If I ever truly become
one of those "nice" ones,
then don't ever feel
any guilt of walking away
and cutting me out of your life,
for I was the one who wronged you,
not the other way around

## May Be

I know you think it's a trap
meant to break you,
meant to teach you
that no one could feel
that way about you,
but maybe it's not
maybe this is the real thing

Maybe you never wanted
to feel a thing,
maybe you didn't want your heart
to sing their name,
but maybe
that's something your
heart gets to decide,
bypassing the brain
and it's the strict laws
of emotional control,
and maybe you
can't logic yourself out of this one

Maybe you don't think
you deserve to be seen
and admired,
maybe you don't think
you deserve someone
who treats you with respect,
maybe you don't think
you deserve to be
treated as an equal,
maybe you don't think
you deserve love,
but maybe there's something
inside you that knows better

Maybe some part of you
loves you,
some part of you
knows you deserve love

## Attention

Boy, oh boy,
aren't you sweet?
I'm glad we had
the chance to meet

Whether this keeps up
or falls to bits,
either way
I'll appreciate the
boost of self-esteem
your attention has given me

And all I really wanted,
despite all the admiration
you've passed my way,
day after day,
was a little attention,
a little affection,
before I rambled on
to some other thing,
to some other fling

# Pretend

As I stared into your eyes
during the passing of a fiery
twilight,
drinking in the
summery scent of your skin,
and the look of autumn in your hair,
I realized that maybe it's time
to let myself fall off the top,
all the way down
to the watery rocks below,
and let the crashing waves
erode away whatever walls
didn't completely smash
on my way to falling in love

I am not one who willingly gives in,
but you're one who's worth it
for me to play pretend,
as if I knew this could all last
longer
than the time it took for you
to lock eyes with another

You were someone
I would have happily
wasted the rest of my life with

## Unrequited

I pined away for you,
day after day,
hoping you'd look my way
with that certain gaze

I had a net at the ready
to catch your heart,
should you have decided
to set it free

Hoping can only get you so far
when you take no action,
and say little to nothing
but you turned the other way,
and I took it as a sign

Now I'm left with all the love I had
to give
And once again,
my feelings are left unrequited

# Be Bold

With this magic I hold,
I cast a spell to be bold,
for I haven't the nerve
to speak my heart's desire,
for being near you
causes me to perspire,
and makes the words
escape my tongue with
a quiver and a shake,
with little grace to mask
my mistakes

If I can't find the power
to speak to you without fear,
If I can't be bold,
how can I ever expect to win
your heart?

# Breath Reads Salty

Your breath reads salty,
like the sea,
as it laps against my lips,
colliding as if
waves against the sandy shore

Then, your presence,
like cool, dark water,
washes over me,
sending shivers down my spine,
recalling to me
thoughts of the ocean
and the depths unexplored

Had I gills,
I'd stay under forever

# Little Shelf Inside My Heart

There's a shelf inside my heart,
sitting before a window,
half empty, cleared, dusted,
and ready for use

If you'd like
you can use it,
placing your memories
right beside mine,
our items fading in the sun together
through yellowed lace curtains,
figurines shimmering
in the moonlight,
posed to dance

The little shelf inside my heart
will always have room
for me and you,
no matter how much we pile on
so we don't have to pick and choose
what we bring,
we can always rearrange
whenever the need rises

And wouldn't it be lovely?
The little shelf inside my heart,
decorated with touches of our love,
bringing a shine to a room
lacking in decoration

## Hollyhock for Your Heart

A hollyhock for your heart,
that's all I can offer.
It's as red as a rose
yet lacks the romance,
and like a camellia
it lacks any sweet scent.
But it's meaning…
I hope you take it all the same

A hollyhock for your heart,
for I couldn't find a carnation
to say how you are my fascination,
or pluck a sunflower
to convey that you are
the light of my day.
Daffodils only laugh
at the token I have chosen
to exchange for your admiration.
They know I am not a true knight
and doubt I was ever the cause
of a butterfly's flight.

Dandelions will only blow
away my wishes into the wind.
An aster may prove my patience,
but honestly, who has time for that?
An Iris, well, I have not the class
to hand it to such a lovely soul

It is a token of my affections,
just that and nothing more
for I lack the sense of fashion
to show you that kind of passion.
I really can't afford much more...

All I can offer
is a hollyhock for your heart

## Drunken Text

Here I am,
all alone,
sitting exposed,
body and soul,
aching for your consolation,
but it's past midnight,
and you're in bed,
and I'm completely out of my head

I'm sending a million drunken texts
with heartfelt laments
In the morning,
I know I'll be full of regrets,
but in this moment,
my booze filled sentiments are
spilling over,
and rending my heart to bits

And after this final drunken text,
I'll carry myself off to bed
and fall into a dizzying sleep
full of snippets of dreams
and little comfort

## Preference

Love is love,
and no one else
has a right to say
what your preference should be

It's something you feel
from within,
something you feel
within your heart

And with time,
preferences may change
and with time,
they may stay the same

It still doesn't change
that love is love,
and no one else
has a right to say
who you do,
and who you don't,
get to love,
and want to love,
romantic or platonic,
monogamous or polyamorous,
nobody else can say
for you but you

# Broken Love

*Poems about broken love and broken hearts*

## When Hearts are Broken

When hearts are broken,
cuts and slashes rip into
the surface and burrow
their way down into your core
and you feel
that you can't love anymore

When hearts are broken,
you're more than sure
that it could never be fixed,
that the cracks
will keep expanding
until you fall apart

When hearts are broken
you find that not all glues
are meant to mend such things,
but a bit of liquid gold can
fill the splits,
bringing beauty to the pain,
repairing the broken
with the spirit of remembrance,
never forgetting,
but pushing forth,
moving forward

When hearts are broken,
some things seem lost,
never to be found again,
but really, it's your heart
making room for something new,
after tears are shed,
and initial mournings have passed

When hearts are broken
you find yourself hoping
that you'd never be so foolish
to fall in love again

But honestly,
I hope you are foolish
enough to try it again

# They Whisper

There were the ghosts of a whisper
that they used to be lovers,
they'd smooch on the moon
and serenade one another
till the break of day

There were the ghosts of a whisper
that they clasped hands
and used to dance
to the rhythm in their hearts,
in the ballrooms they built

But it's been long since
the moon sunk into the sea
and the sun rose in its place,
and it's been long since
their ballrooms tumbled
down into the ground,
crumbled into dust

They pass each other on
the streets,
and their eyes never meet,
as if the other never existed

And yet, the ghosts,
they whisper of the things
they used to do,
of who they used to be

# For the Sake of You

I do not wish for my pain
to cloud the taste on your tongue
nor to soak up the last of the sun.
You have such little light,
And it grows smaller still.
I can't take that away just
to complain.

So my dear, my starlight's breath,
don't mind me when
I'm in an agitated state,
when you can hear the snap
of a lobster's claw in each
syllable I sing.
I keep it all inside to help
you hold down your worries.
Don't mind me, I'm fine.

I do not wish for my pain
to cause waterfalls to spill
over your face,
and drown your smile of grace,
at least not for my sake.
You're more important.
Or so that's what you've told me.
So I'll sit back and listen to you,
as I always do.

## Once Upon a Time

Once upon a time
in a land known as my mind
I thought love to be a dying cause,
it was just a barrier
to all my ambitions,
and I put up walls on all sides
of my heart,
and build them up every chance
I felt I had to

Once upon a time
I thought love
to be a disease,
or just another hormonal twitch,
you were far away,
and I wasn't alright,
and I didn't want to fall,
Ever.

Once upon a time,
you came into my life
you were mine,
and you taught me
that there was more to life
than anger and pain
You tried to climb those walls
over and over again,
but I kept building higher and higher,
and you felt your heart breaking
more and more
each time you fell down

Once upon a time
just as I thought I'd give
love a chance,
build a door
to the inside of my heart,
you left and never came back,
broken, battered, and bitter,
and I knew that this was
the consequences of the
fortified barriers I made
that let nothing in

# Crash

I'm trying to break free,
but you won't let me go,
gripping me by the inner psyche,
and dragging me down
until I am trapped within
a dark room built by you

What can I do
to escape this prison?
What can I say
to get you to stop?

My love muscle
has been gutted out
and locked inside
your heart shaped box

At first, I didn't mind,
letting your needles
pierce my veins
with your kisses full of promise,
and words that seemed
so sugar sweet,
I never suspected that beneath
your ashen, streaky skin,
that you'd be capable of inflicting
so many pock-marked scars

But I see so much clearer
now that I've refused to play
your love drug addled games

And yet, I feel must
be coming down,
I'm dizzy, woozy, sweating-
from the thought of escape-
but what other choice
is there to make?

If we carry on this way,
I'm going to crash.
Hello floor, into you I smash

## Wings

I was always afraid of flying until
you offered me a place
beneath your wings

From there, oh!
Did we ascend to such great heights,
We danced amongst the clouds,
twirling within the golden lights
of the sunset.
The music of the stars
was ours, and ours alone.
The moon shone with envy
at the sight of our flight

But then, out of nowhere
our shared skies
cracked in half,
never meant to cement.
Your wings fell into a fray
as your feathers molted away,
and your hands lost their grip

Without your wings,
I fell astray.
Into the ground, I smashed.
My heart hardly survived the crash

Locked on the ground,
I felt heavy with doubt,
now that you were no longer around
to hoist me up above
the gravity of my own emotion

It was only after some time,
When I finally settled myself on soil
did end my innermost turmoil
as I realized that I didn't need
your wings to lift me up,
that I needed to do the work myself

It was only with time
that my heart flew free,
and I learned how to
handle my darkness,
and off I soared into the clouds
and the twinkling stars above

Without your loss,
I may have never known
just how far I could have flown

## Shut Your Mouth

Your take on the alphabet
is malnourished, at best,
and I can't stand to hear you speak,
every word sounds as if
you're gnawing on bones

So shut your mouth,
and chew your words,
swallow those bitter letters,
choke on the vowels,
the consonants acting as chalky water,
that's all you get to wash it down

What's left here
is a disgusting display,
your wishes and wants
are rubbish strewn all
across the kitchen floor,
and a sink piled high
with greasy plates and bowls
with your crusty
food for thoughts caked on
Those dishes aren't going
to wash themselves,
so lift up your sleeves
and get to work

I'm sick of you,
I'm done with it.
You can dine alone
for all I care

After today,
I won't have to wipe
your spittle and crumbs
of off my face

## A Million Reasons

I could tell you
a million reasons
as to why and why not,
but I'd rather not
waste another breath

I've catered to your
comfort time and time again,
I went out of my
way just to make
your day, and yet,
it never seems
I have done enough

I didn't know you
were a god-like being,
requiring constant compliments
and ritualistic offerings
in the form of my time,
my money, and
any bits of my soul that fall off

But I know it's never your fault,
terrible things have happened
to you,
and you don't have to be responsible
for your actions as a result,
you can live your live as you please,
diminishing and disregarding,
gaslighting manipulations,
taking and taking,
till the end of your days

I won't stop you,
but I won't be a part of it
any longer

## Heart Eater

When we were together
the air smelled like
rose petals wafting on by,
giving the air such a sweet scent,
masking the foul stench
of what was to come

Oh, those sweet-smelling days
before the corpses started
their promenade!

And then one day,
you carved out my heart,
and devoured it whole,
and left me,
gasping and bleeding,
on the side of the road

I turn into a dried-out husk,
a hungering monster calling
for the love I was denied,
for the heart that was mine,
for the emptiness that now resides

Behind me I left a trail
of other zombified beings
who once fell in love
with a monster who
hid behind a mask
made of sweetness and
well concocted lies

Those poor bastards
never saw it coming,
never knew that I
was a heart eater too

For every heart I devoured,
my hunger only grew,
and no matter what I tried to do,
I was forever cursed to consume

Oh heart eater,
why did you choose me to be doomed

## Into Dust

The memories
we've shared are crushed
into dust beneath
our angry feet

As they are blown away
into the breeze,
there's still a sparkle
that we both see
but refuse to mention to the other

And after it's all gone,
after we can't think
of anymore memories to destroy,
we turn away and go separate ways,
leaving that to be the last
thing we ever did together

## The Inevitable

```
Ropes were tied tight,
but the fibers grew soggy
in the water we waded through

Then came the inevitable snap

After the snap,
we clasped hands,
thinking we could make it past,
but then the floods came,
the currents washed
us separate ways
```

## Finished Plate

Even some of the most
beautiful souls have
a bottomless hunger
that can never be satiated

They will eat you up
with nary a second thought
And whatever bits of you
they deem hard to swallow,
they will force you to cook
yourself into something else,
into something they can stomach,
until you are nothing
but a finished plate,
licked clean,
without a scrap left in sight

## Sweet Tea

You seem sweet like southern tea,
but you're bad for my teeth,
your sugars clog my arteries,
your acclaimed lemony twist
added no real flavor to the taste

At first, I enjoyed
the off flavor,
not one to refuse
a cool drink on
a hot summer day,
but eventually,
seasons change,
even if you stayed the same

You were all sweetness on the surface,
but poison deep within

# Through the Shards of My Heart

Through the shards of my heart,
I write, fingers covered in ink,
painting the truths of my words,
and the truth is,
I've loved you all this time,
I no longer try to find you,
but the love hasn't stopped

Through the shards of my heart,
I clean the mirrored surfaces
to get a better picture of
my memories of you,
I smile at our good times,
and sometimes I wonder what
really could have gone wrong,
besides all the manipulations,
and the disrespect
we passed back and forth,
and the heavy expectations we held
over each other's heads

Through the shards of my heart,
I tried every way to make it work
I wasn't afraid of change,
but I didn't want to change into
what you wanted me to become,
to be something I'm not,
I wanted to be a better version of me

Through the shards of my heart,
I'll write of your inner beauty,
paint pictures of your inner beast,
I didn't always understand you,
but through these arts,
I can move forward
and make something of myself

And through the shards of my heart
I'll pray you find your way,
and with time,
I hope you can forgive me,
and maybe I can forgive you, too

## Drunken Knight

My drunken knight,
stumbling and bumbling
through alleyways
and dark streets,
puking up their guts,
before barreling into
a fight with a stranger,
whose face seemed
just a little too funny,
whose comments seemed
to be targeted their way

Your calls after midnight
have no end,
keeping me from sleep

I wish to resign
from this position
of pick-me-ups and caretaker,
but we both know
that as soon as you call,
I'll be there to take you home

I keep thinking of the days
when you wore the best armor
in the land,
and won every joust,
and I always think
that you could do it again,
if only I help you better yourself,
if only I hold on just a little longer

## Meant to Be

You're not the one that
I thought you were,
or was it…
that you weren't the
one that I wanted you to be?

And I'm not the one
you thought I was,
or the one you wanted me to be.

That was a glamor I wore
over my gremlin face plate,
hiding secrets, hiding selfs

We were never the people
we wanted to be,
whether it be that
we were together or not,
but maybe after all,
it's better this way

Now we can be
who we are meant to be,
and be with people
who help us feel free

# Letting the Love Be

*When love is real, healthy, and hopeful*

## Love, At Last

Avast! There it be!
Love, at long last!
Love for me!

I've searched all the
islands in the sea,
followed every map
that claimed
they could lead me
to the treasure there could be

But no legends held true,
and fell through did every clue,
to find the love I longed for

Until I threw caution to the wind
and tried something new
did I finally find
the map that led me to you

I unfurled the sails
and followed the trail
until I reached those golden shores

I dug down into the spot,
and fell into the hidden cave
where you stayed,
and once we locked eyes,
I knew it was love,
love, at last

## I Found You

The flowers may not bloom
in a world fully doomed
but who needs them when
I've got your
earthen eyes of a beautiful hue
to look upon when a lack
of vegetation and color
plagues the land

Though I have many things
I want to do,
and elder years I wish to live,
I'm not too worried about
how and when
I'll meet my end
because in this life,
I found you,
and have felt the greatest love
I have ever felt

# Don't Want the Music to Stop

The harp players
pluck at the chords
of our hearts,
playing a song
of me and you

I feel as if
I were dancing on the moon
as I listen to the tune
of me and you

I can't predict
how the rest of the melody plays,
and I can't always keep my feet
in time with the beat,
but I don't ever want the music to
stop

## Walking in the Rain

Do you remember
walking in the rain
on that cold October day,
while the ducks flew away,
and the trees leaned in to
hear what we had to say,
while we wandered off course,
adventure being the big theme
of that gray, rainy day

I remember.
How could I possibly forget
the way we traded scarves
and caught each other's colds
before finding home,
sitting close, snuggling down
to movies, soup, and hot chocolate

## Triskeles

I don't quite believe in soul mates,
as I don't believe that there
is only one soul out there
that perfectly meshes with mine,
but I can't deny that you and I
are tied together throughout time

Long ago, we must have tied a rope,
a single strand made into a knot,
cementing our lifetimes
to intertwine endlessly
via a triskeles

I don't know what kind
of spell was cast,
to make this last,
but I'm glad it happened

In the perpetual motion of life,
we will always find one another,
time after time,
life after life,
in one form or another

## Hearth

As I look into your eyes,
I find a fire roaring
in the hearth on
a chilly Autumn night

Your warmth is ever
inviting, ever enticing,
especially to a weary traveler
such as me

I may just stay a spell,
stoke the flames as needed
as long as you let me
sit by your hearth
whenever I'm cold

Together, I think we've got a chance,
I don't think the fire
in this hearth will ever go out

## Reassurance

Somedays you come through
like the rays of the summer sun,
that dances through my eyelids
and into my heart,
and on those days,
there's never any uncertainty
that you love me

Other days,
your words fade out like
a figure walking into a heavy fog,
and my doubts cast shadows
that darken my vision,
and raise suspicion
that I'm nothing to you
but a burden,
that you never really loved me
at all

And on those days,
all I need is a little reassurance
to throw out the doubts,
and banish the darkness
that gathered around the
edges of my heart

Let me know
that you've meant all that you said
just a few words
to get me out of my head

Those little gestures,
the reassurances,
mean everything to
someone like me

## Locks

At first,
eyes lock,
then hands, lips, hips…

Lives intertwine,
cells collide,
then divide,
blood thickens,
flows,
organs grow

Two hearts turn the key
to make one beat
whose little bleep
reverberates throughout
every life it ever touches

Life unlocks
with the click
of many locks

## Green Love

Out of her heart grew
little sprouts
and they grew strong
and green,
for him

As they spent time together
the sprouts continued to prosper,
and soon blooms blossomed,
and the fruits of their new love
grew and ripened

As they cared for the sprouts,
the harvests kept coming,
and the green love
nourished them through
those times of smiles
and those times of darkness
throughout the rest of their days

## Vulnerability

There's something about vulnerability
that for so long,
I just didn't understand

I didn't see why
I had to have it,
had to let people in

Eventually,
I had to learn the hard way,
as you just had to get under my skin,
and no amount of coaxing,
no amount pleading,
no amount of trying to shake you,
could get you out

And now, here I am,
sharing with you the
heaviness in my heart,
and the process of my art

I share with you
without the need for approval,
without fear of rejection,
just understanding

I share with you,
with all my love,
my vulnerabilities
with an unspoken promise
that you'll hold them close
and take care of them,
while I do the same for you

## Let the Love Be

Self-sabotager,
let it exist!
Don't snuff it out,
let that spark burn,
let the love be

If you don't stop
casting doubts,
If you don't stop
pushing it away,
it will go
some other way,
and only you are to blame,
Please, just let the love be!

You've waited for this all your life,
for someone who helps you feel whole,
but now you have to do the work
to be better,
instead of falling into old habits
of cutting off all notions of
vulnerability,
now you must do the work
to let the love be

If you let it go,
let it grow,
I can't really say
that the love won't fade,
that you'll make it
until the very end,
but I can say
that it's worth it,
that they're worth it,
so I say,
don't try to stop it,
let the love be

## To the Women I've Loved

To all the women I loved:

I never told you
that I fell in love with you
because I hadn't quite
come to terms with myself

For years and years,
I struggled,
pushing down
my attractions towards you,
believing that it couldn't be,
that for me, it had to be one
or the other

It took me a long time
to accept my truth,
that I could be attracted
to anyone of any gender

Though I worry
that I'll be seen as different,
as some sort of mutant
that doesn't belong,
that's made all wrong,
I'll still stand strong
for what is real,
for the love I feel

What they say may hurt,
but love is stronger and brighter
than bitter words
born of misunderstanding and hatred,
and I am stronger in heart
than they could ever possibly dream

## My Adonis

My Adonis isn't a Grecian god,
nor is he sculpted from stone,
he is made of flesh and bone

Stretch marks and veins
streak across his skin
like rivers and lightning,
and his hips and belly are hillsides
my fingers frolic on as we lay
together,
his eyes are of rich, earthly tones,
shimmering with great love and great
fire

My Adonis may not be
sculpted from stone,
and he may not be without his flaws,
but in my eyes, he is true beauty,
timeless, original, and beyond compare

## Your Patience

Around my heart
I build a stone fortress
with tall walls
and barbed wire

I was more than
prepared to fight
against any that
threatened to conquer
over me and
my emotions

But it didn't
take an army
to make it through the walls

All it took
was your time,
your understanding,
your patience

Eventually I surrendered
and dropped the iron gates,
unlocked all the doors
for you to explore
every bit of me,
and soon, I felt no shame
in your presence

And all it took was your patience

# Acknowledgements and Notes

First off, I would like to say that when it comes to my old poems, I did my best to try and keep the essence of the original while also editing it to make a little more sense. A lot of my old poems didn't really stick with one theme. They had one major theme with several piles on top. There's nothing wrong with that, but for my own poetry, it just didn't really work.

I will say, some of my older poems are a little better than I thought. I have to give myself a little credit, I think. I can see the roots of how I write now within those lines and verses. I'm proud of myself for getting this far. I plan to go even further though!

The poems "Decision on Doors" and "Wings" have also been featured in "Whimsy and Weirdos: Poetry for the Unique" by Andrea Campbell and myself.

Anyways, on to the thanking of the people and the things!

I would really like to thank my wonderful partner, Foster Green. He gave me a lot of advice on design, proofread the poems, and gave me a lot of much appreciated feedback on the cover art and poems. He's always encouraged me in all the things I do.

Also, like, thanks to my mom! This is not only for giving birth to me, but also for being one of the best moms ever.

I would like to thank all my friends for all your support and love as well.

And of course, I would like to thank the two people this book is dedicated to. When I was a kid, I went through a very tough time and these teachers tried extra hard to help me through those dark times. Mrs. Schnieder gave me a beautiful green notebook with butterflies on it. She encouraged me to write, since I seemed to enjoy it so much.

Mr. Tim was the school guidance counselor. When I was having bad days, he let me go into his office whenever I needed to, even on days when I was too upset to speak. He would sit with me in my darkened state as long as I needed it.

While I lost contact with them not long after I moved to a different town after that school year, I still think of them often. I hope they are doing well.

And, of course, an extra special thank you to all of you beautiful readers. Thank you for giving me a chance!

# About the Author

Machelle Berglund grew up on the wild plains of Southeastern South Dakota. She enjoys writing, painting, drawing, playing video games, and playing Dungeons and Dragons with her friends. She is a proud alum of the Americorps NCCC program and enjoys helping others whenever she can. She currently resides in Brookings, SD with three cats, a ferret, her partner, and a corn snake named Cornelius.

Machelle is also co-author, along with Andrea Campbell, of Whimsy and Weirdos: Poetry for the Unique.

Printed in the USA
CPSIA information can be obtained
at www.ICGtesting.com
LVHW010853100924
790299LV00008B/144